GETTYSBURG

Civil War Memories

I · N · S · I · G · H · T · S

BOOKS

Harrisburg, PA

Ruth Hoover Seitz

Photography by Blair Seitz

Cover: Monument honors the 8th Regiment of the Pennsylvania Cavalry, Gettysburg National Military Park.
Page 1: In Gettysburg National Military Park a monument honoring the 72nd Pennsylvania Infantry stands east of the stone wall over which Pickett's men surged.
This page: A cannon used by the Army of the Potomac is now silent in Gettysburg National Military Park.

INTRODUCTION

During three days of intense fighting between Union and Confederate troops in July of 1863, Gettysburg residents and battle participants experienced upheaval and destruction beyond the wildest imagination. Those who survived shared their experiences for years afterward. People with the foresight of historian J. Howard Wert gathered accounts and battle-field memorabilia. In their recollections are sharp feelings and graphic images of their community under the impact of the costliest battle of the Civil War. A boy's description or a young lady's observations offer their perceptions of what happened in this rural Pennsylvania town.

In this book you can glean new insight from C. M. McCurdy's Gettysburg: A Memoir recently found in the renowned J. Howard Wert Gettysburg Collection. McCurdy's fresh and clear narrative tells how he, a man in his seventies, remembers what it meant to have thousands of soldiers pour into town and disrupt his boyhood. You can watch his ten-year-old adventure-

GETTYSBURG

Civil War
Memories

Text © 1996 by Ruth Hoover Seitz
Photography © 1996 by Blair Seitz
ISBN 1-879441-01-2
Library of Congress Catalog Card
Number 95-92703

Published by

RB
BOOKS

Seitz and Seitz, Inc.
1006 N. Second Street
Harrisburg, PA 17102-3121
Phone 717 232-7944

BOOKS ™

Harrisburg, PA
Ruth Hoover Seitz
Photography by Blair Seitz
Designed by Klinginsmith & Company
Printed in PA, USA

some view of war dim. You can observe clever-
ness in assuring family safety. His observations of battle repercussions gain support
from other civilian accounts which run
parallel as excerpts.

This book features color photographs of
battle relics from the J.H. Wert Gettysburg
Collection, available to the eyes of the public
for the first time in this century.

We appreciate those who helped with this
project. Many thanks to G. Craig Caba of
the Harrisburg Civil War Round Table;
Dr. Richard J. Sommers, Chief Archivist
Historian, Archives, U.S. Army Military
History Institute, Carlisle Barracks
and James E. Schmick, a
founder of the Camp Curtin Historical
Society. We are grateful to those who
assisted us at the Gettysburg National
Military Park Library and the Adams
County Historical Society, both in
Gettysburg. These pages benefit from
research by Christie Morrison and Laura M.
King, Dickinson College interns. We appre-
ciate permission to photograph artifacts in
the Wert Gettysburg Collection.

Gettysburg: A Memoir
by Charles M. McCurdy

Charles M. McCurdy was elderly when he wrote about the Battle of Gettysburg which he experienced as a ten-year-old. What he remembers as a boy during those days of chaos and uncertainty brings a poignant realism to his interpretation of war coming to his hometown of approximately 2,400 people in rural Pennsylvania. McCurdy's boyish longing for adventure was more than satisfied by the events of July 1, 2 and 3 of 1863.

A view from a tower in Gettysburg National Military Park shows the countryside that was impacted by the Battle in 1863.

Battle Premonitions

It seems strange that the presence of Confederate troops did not suggest to the people the possibility of a battle nearby. Gettysburg was a center from which ten highways radiated. Later it was known that Lee had ordered his army to concentrate there. The local topography was strikingly adapted to the evolution of troops...

Many years after the battle I was talking with the Reverend Dr. Paxton, President of Princeton Theological Seminary, who had been reared near Gettysburg and was a frequent visitor. Dr. Paxton said

"On June 30, 1863 the 17th Pennsylvania was the leading regiment in our division and the first command of the Army of the Potomac to enter Gettysburg. The citizens cheered us greatly and gave us other substantial evidences that we were welcome."
—H.P. Moyer, bugler, 17th PA Cavalry

"The appearance of the soldiers in blue was hailed by the citizens.... As they passed along Washington Street... lassies stood on the corners singing patriotic songs and waved flags."
—J. Howard Wert, historian who lived in Gettysburg at the time of the battle

A "large star" flag waved by Emma Letitia Aughinbaugh when the 17th PA Cavalry arrived in Gettysburg. The bugle (Klemm), spurs and horseshoe medal, the unit's symbol, belonged to the regiment's bugler.

that one evening a year or two before the war he was sitting on Cemetery Hill, looking at the beautiful country about him and sadly thinking how the peace and quiet of this lovely landscape might be destroyed by war, for the tension between the North and South had almost reached the breaking point. He thought how near Gettysburg was to the border, of the highways that offered avenues of easy approach, and how the broad plains before him, flanked on either side by great ridges, seemed to offer an ideal ground for battle. It seemed, in the light of events, almost like a prophecy fulfilled.

Yet it does not seem that people realized the possibility of a battle at their doors. No restriction was placed on my goings and comings. I was not warned to keep near home.

On the afternoon of

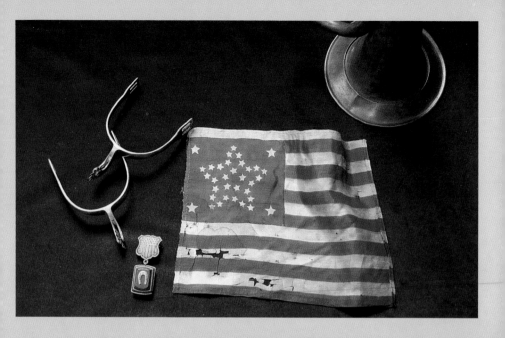

June 30, 1863, a long line of blue-clad cavalry armed with pistol, saber and carbine rode into Gettysburg from the south. Passing through the town, they encamped a half mile to the northwest.

Three weeks before, Lee with the Army of Northern Virginia had begun his forward movement into Pennsylvania... While [Brig. Gen. John] Buford, [commander of the Union's First Division, Cavalry Corps] with two brigades of cavalry rode into Gettysburg–in advance of the main body of the Army of the Potomac–the hosts of the Confederacy were pouring through the mountain roads that led into the country on his front. When night fell this entire region, many miles in extent, was filled with Confederate troops.

On the morning of July 1, Buford, having

CLOSE CALL

"During the afternoon of the first day's battle my father and sister were talking to a Union soldier during a lull in the fighting in front of our house. The soldier was hit by a glancing ball. Being surprised he turned toward where the ball came, then calmly cut the damaged button from his uniform with a common pocket knife. He stated to my sister, 'Young ladies are fond of such souvenirs,' as he handed over the brass button. He returned to his military duties north of town never to be seen again."

—recollection of Mrs. J. Howard Wert (Emma Letitia Aughinbaugh) as written by her son Howard Houck Wert

Photo of Emma L. Aughinbaugh (1845-1909) with the dented button given to her younger sister Nellie by a Union soldier.

discovered the enemy, dismounted his men and moved forward as infantry. He soon was fiercely attacked by the advancing Confederates and the Battle of Gettysburg began.

At the time of the battle I was ten years old. Rather young for any unusual experience.

What now surprises me, when I recall my experiences, is the matter of fact way in which I looked on this tremendous event. Like most boys I found, as Stevenson has said, "that the world is full of a number of things," and some of the most unimportant of these things I would expend the full measure of my emotion.

The battle was too big for a little boy. Had I realized that the noise and tumult, the confusion and excitement that continued for three days meant that 140,000 men were trying to kill each other—using the

Above: Still a thoroughfare and home to Gettysburg residents today. Chambersburg Pike was familiar territory to ten-year-old McCurdy in 1863.

deadly machinery of war so effectively that, at the end of the third day, almost one third of those actually engaged were either killed or more or less horribly mangled—my emotion might have been more in keeping with the great tragedy. But my ideas of war were gained from seeing bright young men

wearing coveted uniforms and
bearing coveted arms, for many
Union soldiers had passed
through Gettysburg during the
preceding years; and from
reading Abbott's *Life of
Napoleon*, Scott's *Campaigns in
Mexico*, romances that I discovered in our garret in some old
numbers of *Harper's* Magazine.

Historian J. Howard Wert wrote: "This is but a specimen of the losses in officers in many Confederate commands engaged on July 1st. General Iverson reported: 'When I saw white handkerchiefs raised and my line of battle still lying down in position, I characterized the surrender as disgraceful, but when I found afterwards that 500 of my men were lying dead and wounded in a line as straight as a dress parade, I exonerated the survivors and claim for the brigade that they nobly fought and died.' Gen. Iverson's North Carolina brigade reported killed and wounded,

These seemed to make war a splendid and glorious adventure. So the tragedy was not present—only little incidents connected with it.

My wildest dreams of adventure did not include a battle. I had had successful encounters with pirates and Indians, and wild animals, but when I found myself running away from the sound of booming cannon and the sight of bursting shells, as fast as my little legs could carry me, the experience far exceeded anything I had imagined. No wonder I did not realize its import.

ONLY SIX MILES FROM THE MASON-DIXON LINE

From the beginning of the war we had been expecting Rebel raids. We lived only a short day's drive from the Potomac, which seemed to be the dividing line between North

458 and captured, 308 the first

day of battle."

In Iverson's pits, as the trench graves

of his men were called, were found

numerous relics, including a fur

haversack, Tranter revolver, a white

plantation officer's vest with blood

stain, a silver engraved snuff box and

a leather-covered canteen.

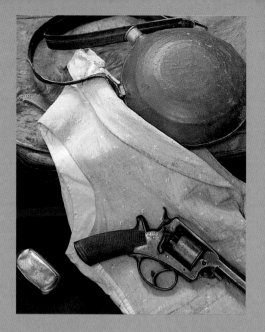

Above: Relics found in trench graves of Gen. Alfred Iverson's men.

and South. Although Maryland had not seceded, many of her men were in the Southern army and sentiment for the South was strong. We knew that there were certain brilliant Confederate cavalry officers who loved to do spectacular things, who wore plumes in their hats and affected a dress that revealed a love for romantic exploits.

A raid into rich and opulent Pennsylvania, which the war had only enriched, would not only add to their renown for daring deeds but would yield a more substantial reward in horses and supplies badly needed by the enemy. Amateur scouts patrolling the roads that led to the river would now and then produce hostile troopers from very unlikely sources. Then would come the wild dash for the valley and the cry "The Rebels are coming." Instantly there was a wild scurry by

Veterans at the Battle's 50th anniversary decided to create a lasting symbol of national unity. This Eternal Light Peace Memorial was dedicated July 3, 1938, the 75th anniversary.

No Gourmet Dishes For the Starving

"The rags and hunger of the Confederate soldiers was always a pathetic story to Mother. She said, 'The stores were closed, but the Confederates broke all of them open and helped themselves to the contents. They were so starved that I have seen them knock the tops from kegs of salt mackerel, snatch the fish from the brine, and eat them,—heads, tails and all.'

"That was more than Mother could stand. She would tell the men to give her the fish to broil ... for them. Mother would say those poor fellows were

every owner of a horse to get it out of the way of danger. Farmers who lived near the mountains easily found safe hiding places in ravines remote from the public roads. Others hurried with their steeds to safe havens beyond the Susquehanna. Other livestock was left to its fate but horses moved quickly and were precious in the eyes of their owners.

    One farmer in the fall of '62 brought a four-horse load of apples into town for sale. He had scarcely begun his sale when an alarm was sounded. Without a moment's delay he unhitched his horses and mounting one, led the others as fast as possible towards the east. I think he made some futile effort to save his fruit, but an unprotected four-horse wagon load of apples was a windfall that seldom comes to boys and they made the most of it.

somebodies' sons, and she could not stand it to see them eat the fish

uncooked.... They would grab it like animals.

"'I have seen them take packages of baking soda out of the store, open

a parcel of it and eat it.'"

—*Louis Dale Leeds in an account about her mother, Nellie E. Aughinbaugh.*

PRECAUTIONS BY BUSINESSMEN

Merchants in town kept their choicest goods in form convenient for quick shipment. Several times the bank cashier packed his cash and valuables into a valise, locked up his institution and joined the departing throng. To be in the fashion, I kept my most cherished possessions in a little box, ready for shipment, feeling quite important at the thought of danger. But I suspect that the most hardened looter would not have found there anything to interest him.

Finally the thing we had so long expected, and that the small boys had hoped for, happened. Word came that Rebel cavalry really was coming in by Chambersburg Pike. Instantly, on hearing the thrilling news I ran down to the end of the street by which they would enter town. A little crowd of old men and boys had gathered and all were anxiously looking towards Seminary Ridge which hid from view the road beyond. One boy had a little cannon made from a piece of gas pipe about fifteen inches long. One end was hammered flat and a touch hole filed, and mounted

on a block of wood it made a noisy, if not very accurate piece of ordnance. He had fired his gun and was preparing to repeat the salute when he was stopped by the men who told him that coming Rebels might think we were shooting at them and return the fire with unpleasant results.

Precious Moments

At the age of 87, Emma Yount Stumpf (1856-1946) wrote a letter to her family telling the following experience that happened when she was age seven playing outdoors in Gettysburg.

"On the evening before the Battle at Gettysburg the streets and pavements were crowded with Soldiers. One who was sitting on our doorstep asked me to come and talk to him. He then told me he had a little Girl at home, and that on the coming day there would be a great battle fought, and he might

Men in Gray Arrive

We had not long to wait. Soon over the brow of the hill came horses with riders in gray. I waited only for the front line to come into view, near enough to see that they really were what I had hoped to see, and making record time struck for home, which was on their line of march, and stationing myself on the front porch, watched the spectacular entry.

In a few minutes up the street they came at a gallop, firing their pistols and giving the Rebel yell. Yet it was not as thrilling as I had expected. This was no wild unrestrained Mazeppa-like rush—rather a leisurely and gentle canter exacted from reluctant and protesting horses. The pistols were fired in the air, the yelling sounded half-hearted and altogether it lacked dramatic effect. I do not know why they made *never see his little Girl again. He asked me if I would kiss him for her sake, so I said I would go ask my Mother and she said, Yes, under the circumstances I could do so, which I did. He then gave me a beautiful silk handkerchief. The border was striped in red, white and blue and in the center was a picture of the head of Washington. I kept this as a treasure all these years.... It is but natural that we would all like to know if the Soldier ever returned to his little Girl, or if he sleeps in that beautiful cemetery at Gettysburg."*

this display. Probably it was to induce the belief that they were rather desperate fellows so that the demand for money and supplies, which quickly followed, would be met.

Although I remember seeing only this small force of cavalry, one of the three corps comprising the Army of Northern Virginia was near, and soon after Mr. Kendlehart, the burgess, received a note from General Ewell, the Confederate commander, demanding $10,000 in cash and certain supplies. The burgess replied saying that on the news of their coming the cashier of the bank had gone off with all the cash, that he knew of no other source from which it could be had, neither could he meet the demand for supplies. This reply closed the incident.

Some years later the colonel of one of Lee's Virginia Regiments said to me, "Lee

Battle Trauma Among Residents

"Nearly all the afternoon it seemed as if the heavens and earth were crashing together. The time that we sat in the cellar seemed long, listening to the terrific sound of the strife,... We knew that with every explosion, and the scream of each shell, human beings were hurried, through excruciating pain, into another world, and that many more were torn, and mangled, and lying in torment worse than death, and no one able to extend relief. The thought made me very sad."

–Sallie Robbins Broadhead, a Gettysburg resident, in her July 1, 1863 diary entry

went north to get shoes for his army." Certainly these cavalrymen looked as if they needed not only shoes but other proper equipment. Their uniforms of dull, uninteresting gray were worn and shabby, showing signs of long and hard wear. They rode into the public square and dismounted and soon I was hobnobbing with them, finding them very charming and friendly, showing the feeling of protective comradeship that nice young men show to little boys. They asked many questions and sent me on errands for things to eat. I am ashamed to say that I did not return with their commissions, for I could not waste the precious moments of their stay for anything as humdrum as bread and butter. They stopped in town but an hour and rode off to join the larger force.

A cannon that was involved in the heaviest artillery fire of the Civil War now stands in silence at Gettysburg.

SWEETS ABUNDANT

Of course all the stores were closed at news of the coming enemy. Doubtless some of them were opened and goods that cavalrymen could carry away taken.

Across the street from our house a little man named Philip Winter kept a cake and candy shop. He was only about five feet high, so very quiet and unobtrusive, minding only his own small affairs, that the children, who were his chief patrons, called him Petey Winters. Only the very forward ventured to address him in this familiar way for he had quiet dignity that resented the use of this diminutive. His specialties were molasses taffy as sticks stuck on bits of brown paper and sold for a penny and... round ginger cakes of great substance.

When it definitely was

BUCKTAIL BRAVERY

The Bucktail brigade of three Pennsylvania regiments (143rd, 149th and 150th) were known for their marksmanship. Wearing a tail of a deer on each soldier's kepi symbolized the famed hunting skills of the Bucktails.

In blazing noon heat on July 1 Col. Langhorne Wister of Duncannon, PA courageously led this brigade. He was shot in the face while giving an order and kept the field, leading a bayonet charge to repulse Confederate advances. Earlier in the day, Wister had accepted the offer of Gettysburg civilian John Burns to join the battle. Burns' fearlessness became legendary.

known that the Rebels were coming Mr. Winter locked his front door, closed his wooden shutters, fastening them with diagonal iron bars, and retired to the privacy of his apartments in the rear of his shop. But the invaders learned that behind these iron bars there was a stock of sweets. Mr. Winter was brought to the front, his door was opened, and soon a perplexed little man was overwhelmed with orders. No penny sales of molasses taffy now. He was doing the business of his life, handing out candy in exchange for Confederate money.

One big trooper came out of the shop with his hat full of candy and seeing an expectant looking small boy gazing enviously at his store gave me a handful. How often during the years that have passed have I thought of that kindly youth. How often have I hoped that

A SAVING RESPONSE

"Just before the action [of the second day] General Meade sent me to the left to examine the condition of affairs and I continued to Little Round Top. It was used only as a signal station. I saw that this was the key to the whole position. Our troops in the woods in front of it could not see the ground in front of them; therefore the enemy would be upon them before they would be aware.

"The woods west of the Emmitsburg road furnished a concealed place for the enemy to form, so I requested a battery just in front of Little Round Top to fire a shot into those woods. The sound of the shot whistling through the air reached the enemy's troops, causing them to glance up in that direction. This

he, and a young Union officer who helped me get a sword, as I shall presently relate, did not share the fate of so many thousands who a week later met their death on the fields around Gettysburg.

When I heard that a great force of Union Cavalry was coming in by the Emmitsburg road, I ran out to meet them. I remember that cherries were ripening and I had a branch filled with the beautiful red fruit which was more alluring to the eye than to the palate, but which helped satisfy the craving that all small boys have for fruit of any kind, ripe or unripe. I sat on the top rail of a fence and watched the long procession ride by, the perfectly accoutered troops offering a strong contrast to the Rebel cavalry I had seen a week before.

After a time I got off my perch and, joining the company

motion revealed to me the glistening gunbarrels and bayonets of the enemy battle line, already formed and far outflanking our troops; his line to advance was unopposed. This discovery was intensely thrilling and appalling...."–G. K. Warren, Gen. George Meade's Chief Engineer, an officer whose quick response saved the Union from losing a strategic hill.

Above: Statue of Gen. G. K. Warren, Chief Engineer of the Army of the Potomac, suggests a keen observer.

of small boys found at the tail end of any procession, trudged alongside the company to their camping place, watching with absorbed interest the putting up of their tents, the simple preparations for supper and all the stir and orderly confusion that attends making camp. It does not appear that any one outside military circles knew that a battle was impending for the next morning.

A PRIZE FIND

I mmediately after breakfast Young McCurdy headed for Buford's camp, but all the soldiers had gone. He decided to turn back to town in search of more excitement when this ten-year-old made a real find.

As I went toward the road I saw an officer's small sword that had been driven into the ground up to the hilt. Here was a prize indeed. I

THE WHEATFIELD

"This was the very 'whirlpool' not only of the second day, but of the entire battle of Gettysburg.

"Where at noon was waving grain, in golden ripeness and luxuriance, the darkness fell on heel-pressed sod that oozed forth blood—on brooklets that ran in crimson streams—on a land so thickly sown with the dying and the dead, that those who traveled on the field walked on corpses....

"At least six times the Confederates rushed across it, sweeping all before them: and, as often, Federal brigades, with a counter-charge, sent them back beaten and dismayed.... No words can portray the awful picture of

Below: Among the hundreds of relics that littered the Wheatfield of the Rose Farm were a homemade straw plantation hat and a South Carolina horse pistol with incised Spanish moss decorating the leather holster.

desolation, devastation and death presented.
"Fences and fruits of the earth had alike disappeared before the withering
[sweep] of destruction. All was a trodden, miry waste, with corpses at
every step, and the thickly littered debris of battle,—broken muskets and
soiled bayonets, shattered ammunition chests and blood defiled
clothing, trodden cartridge-boxes and splintered swords, rifled
knapsacks and battered canteens."
—J. Howard Wert, who walked over the Wheatfield and
other parts of the battlefield many
times during the month of July.

THIS WOMAN'S PLACE

"It would make your hair stand out to be where I have been. How would you like to be in the front rank and have the rear rank load and fire their guns over your shoulder? I have been there myself."

—Rosetta Wakeman who enlisted in August of 1862 as Lyons Wakeman in a letter home. She served disguised as a man until her death from a battle-related disease in 1864.

tried to pull it out but it proved too great a task for my little strength. As I tugged away trying to loosen it, a young officer rode by and seeing my fruitless efforts, got off his horse, pulled out the sword and handed it to me with a smile. Then he mounted and rode over the ridge into the dreadful scene that soon followed.

At this moment cannon began to boom and I had my first experience of war. A shell burst a few hundred yards in front. I ran for the road and when I reached it found my father hurrying towards me. Suspecting where I had gone, as soon as it was known that there would be a battle he had hastened out to find me.

Now the cannonading became stronger. Several shells burst along the Chambersburg road, only a short distance to our right, and we ran for town as fast as we could go. I clung

HELPFULNESS CUT SHORT BY A BULLET

Some accounts have become legendary, for instance that of Gettysburg resident Jennie Wade, who did not live to record her own experiences during the battle.

At her birth on May 21, 1843, the Wade family could not have guessed that their lovely Mary Virginia would have the unfortunate distinction of being the only civilian killed during the Battle of Gettysburg. But the events began to unfold even as seventeen-year old "Jennie" sent her sweetheart and childhood friend Jack off to war. During the long days of his absence, Jennie devoted herself to helping to care for the soldiers who were stationed nearby.

to my sword but as the pace became faster it proved too much of a burden and as we passed a field of growing corn I threw it among the foliage, thinking it would not be seen there, and that I could get it the next day. But the next day swords were no longer a novelty.

SURPRISE APPEARANCE

hile Union officers were urging residents who lived on Chambersburg Street, running east and west, to take to the side streets, the McCurdy family hastily packed a few belongings, carefully locked up their home and headed four blocks to the home of Grandmother McCurdy on Baltimore Street.

Not long after our arrival we heard from passing soldiers that General Reynolds, who had just reached the field hurrying on in advance of his corps, had instantly been killed and that his body had been

This monument of a cannoneer with a rammer stands in the Park's Wheatfield near the Peach Orchard.

When the Battle began, Jennie and her mother baked bread at her sister's home for the soldiers who strayed from the battlefield in search of food. The two women passed the entire first day of the battle in this way and told the soldiers they would feed them again the next day.

On the morning of July 3, 1863, Jennie rose in preparation for another busy day of baking. She gathered the necessary firewood, stoked the fire, and kneaded the dough. After leaving it to rise, Jennie went into the living room for her morning prayer. When she returned to begin kneading again, a stray Confederate bullet followed a haphazard course through the front door and

brought into town. General Reynolds was related to my grandmother through the marriage of her brother to a sister of Robert Fulton, and on learning of his death, although she was ninety years old, she wanted to be taken where he lay, thinking that in some way she might minister to him. But Father persuaded her that it was not possible.

Grandmother, as I have said, was ninety years old. She was a stately lady, still handsome with the flushed cheeks of youth. One day when she was resting in bed two Confederate soldiers suddenly appeared in her room. Rising up in bed, she confronted them with bright eyes, indignant at their intrusion. Instantly they backed out of the door, hats in hand, one of them saying: "Madam, we always respect age."

During the cannonading she was taken to the cellar, a

parlor of the McClellan house. It lodged, however, in the heart of Jennie who stood just inside the kitchen door. The bullet killed her instantly.

strip of carpet laid on the floor and a rocking chair provided, in which she sat in state until the danger was past.

BATTLE CHAOS

While the battle was in full tide, there was heavy cannonading and the musket fire was continuous, making a rattling sound like heavy wagons being rapidly driven over a stony pike, or like hail falling on a tin roof. I remember thinking of this comparison at the time. The streets were full of excited people hearing for the first time the dreadful and alarming sounds of battle, scarcely realizing that the greatest drama man can stage was being played at their doors.

Wounded men still able to walk began to go by on their way to Cemetery Hill at the southern end of the town which had been selected as a rallying point in view of a possible repulse. Soon batches of prisoners appeared on their dreary way to the same goal. These were followed by a larger number in charge of an officer who seemed to be unaware of the selection of Cemetery Hill, and did not know what disposition to make of them. An old gentleman who lived next door suggested that they be put in the jailyard near by. I heard the officer say to him; "Old man, we don't put prisoners

A monument to Maj. Gen. John Reynolds stands along Chambersburg Pike in Gettysburg National Military Park.

of war in jail."

Until about four o'clock the air was filled with the sounds of battle. Suddenly we saw surging up the street a wild and disorganized mob of blue-clad soldiers, most of whom had thrown away their guns, many were without hats and all seemed intent only on escaping some dread and imminent peril. If there is a more thrilling spectacle than an army in frenzied retreat through the narrow streets of a town, I cannot imagine it.

One Hour, Fifty-Five Minutes on July 3

"The third day's artillery at Gettysburg is one of those cases where the power of words is vain. While life lasts it can never pass from the memory of anyone who heard it. Oh! that withering tempest that swept over Cemetery Ridge from the converging fire of 150 cannon!

"Every missile known to English and American gunnery was moaning, shrieking swift sons of deaths. Guns were dismounted; caisson after caisson blown up in quick succession; horses and men disemboweled; gunners, in the act of loading, torn limb from limb." –J. Howard Wert, historian who documented the Battle in his 50th anniversary book.

Ammunition fragments–conical and round shells–as well as part of a U.S. sword, a shattered Colt 44 revolver and a splintered bayonet. The discoloration occurred in trench graves of Gen. Pickett's men.

Soon they had passed and individual Confederate soldiers appeared, but strange to say there was no organized pursuit. These soldiers began searching the houses for Union soldiers whom they thought might be hiding within. A posse stopped before the gate behind which my mother was standing and inquired: "Madam, are there any Yankee soldiers in your cellar?"

"No," she replied, "there are no soldiers in my house." Two were concealed in my grandmother's, and she knew it, but it was not *her* house.

My father took me with him to see how conditions were at home. We found the door still locked, although a dent apparently made by the butt of a musket was shown, and a bullet had lodged in the door frame. Beside the little front porch that occupied half the sidewalk, lay two dead Union

"The fate of Gettysburg hung upon a spider's single thread!" Frank A. Haskell, aide to Brigadier General John Gibbon.

soldiers. I had never before seen a dead man, yet I do not recall that I was shocked, so quickly does war brutalize. The wounded I had seen, the fierce excitement that raged around me, had blunted even my young sensibilities.

We went back for the rest of the family.   Everything was as we had left it in the morning. Although nothing had been disturbed in the house everything in the stable

42.

THE HEROISM OF ABNER WEBB

On July 3, Captain Silas Gardner of Company C, 3rd Wisconsin Infantry,

witnessed an act of heroism as daring as any performed during the War.

" The day was very hot, and there was one man among the

wounded who commenced calling for water. I have heard that cry many times

before and since, but nothing like that one. (He had) an entreaty and pathos

in his voice that would touch a heart of stone. It was maddening. The men all

became nervous, would move uneasily about, and tried to keep up conversation,

but still that cry rang out.

Below: Christ Lutheran Church, situated a half block west of Gettysburg's square, held wounded from the first day of battle. Here the Patriot Daughters nursed soldiers.

had been taken, including two pigs which belonged to Owen Robinson, the colored sexton of the Presbyterian Church.

We were now within the Confederate lines, the repulse of the Union forces on the first day giving them possession of the town. Aside from the despondency this caused, the change made little difference. We went to bed that night weary after a day of excitement and strange adventure, not knowing what to expect on the morrow. For the repulse of the Union forces seemed decisive and we did not know anything beyond what we had seen.

CELLAR SAFETY

I suspect that my capacity for emotion had become exhausted by the excitement of the battle of the first day, for when firing was resumed, it seemed an old story. Cannon

"Soon I saw a member of my company spring to his feet, hasten to the rear and fill his canteen from the spring, come back and take off his accouterments. It was Abner Webb. I asked him what he was going to do. He replied: 'Captain, I can't stand it any longer, I am going to take that man a drink if they shoot the hell out of me.' I called the men into line, and as we sprang over the works, we opened fire, but they did not seem to pay much attention to us, but directed their fire to the unarmed (Abner Webb). He reached the wounded man, and throwing himself on the ground beside him, raised the canteen to the lips of the sufferer and let him drink. After breathing himself a moment,

thundered and musketry fire rattled all day. Much of the time we spent in the cellar which I thought an unnecessary precaution. Whenever there was a lull in the cannonading I was on the street, which provided large entertainment.

Two doors below our house the College Lutheran Church was filled with wounded, as were all the churches and other public buildings. The auditorium of this church was on the second floor and the wounded had to be carried up a long flight of stairs from the street. Surgeons were at work under very rude conditions, and I often have wondered how there could be any recovery from wounds that were dressed without any of the safeguards against infection that modern surgery supplies. The church yard was strewn with arms and legs that had been amputated and thrown out of the windows *leaving the canteen, he started on the return trip. The bullets of the enemy fairly rained around him, even though they could plainly see what he had done. But through that storm of lead he sprang over the works untouched. "With a cheery smile on his face, he said, 'Well, I gave him a drink in spite of them.'"*

and all around were wounded men for whom no place had yet been found. I remember very little about the events of this day, for there was the same dreadful monotony of sound and awful sights of suffering.

By this time I was getting pretty tired of ham. It was the staple dish for we had only makeshift substitutes for bread. But we had apple butter and preserves, and fared well compared with the poor fellows who were being killed and mangled all about us, and whose commissary service during the fighting must have been interrupted.

LAST DAY OF BATTLE

On the morning of the third day there was a repetition of the experiences of the two preceding days. Soon after noon, however, the most terrific cannonading that we

A bonnet, basket, invalid cup and leatherbound Lutheran Bible were owned by Gettysburg resident Katie Wert, who nursed the wounded.

A contemporary reenactment of Barksdale's Charge by "The Fury of Gettysburg" portrays some of the aspects of the fighting of July 2, 1863.

had heard began. As soon as it slackened we came up from the cellar, and Father took me with him to the third floor of our house from which one could look from a dormer window towards the scene of the firing, a mile or more away. A dense volume of smoke hid everything from view, but we could plainly hear through this screen, the Rebel yell and the answering

Union cheer. Weird and inspiring sounds. Soon everything became still, and although we did not know it, the battle had ended with victory for the Union army. At night camp fires twinkled along Seminary Ridge, marking the Confederate line of battle. But only to deceive. Already they had begun their awful retreat, carrying with them over rough and

"At first every house and barn for many miles was a hospital from which came day and night without cessation the shrieks and agony of death. After the battle nine white-walled [tent] cities, stretching over meadowland and forest held 21,300 Union and Confederate wounded."

—*J. Howard Wert*

stony roads thousands of wounded, subject to all the horrors of such a journey.

On the morning of the Fourth of July we still were apprehensive, for the report went about among the citizens that the town was to be shelled. The military authorities soon learned that the danger was past—the battle fought and won.

ENEMIES HEAL IN THE SAME HOUSE

One evening a few days after the battle an ambulance, in charge of two Union soldiers, stopped in front of our house. Father was on the porch and he learned from the men that it contained a wounded Confederate officer who had been ordered sent to Fortress Monroe. The evening trains for Baltimore had gone, and the

AMPUTATION

"...just outside of the yard, I noticed a pile of limbs higher than the fence. It was a ghastly sight! Gazing upon these,... I could have no other feeling, than that the whole scene was one of cruel butchery."

—Tillie Pierce Alleman, a Gettysburg woman

The dress sword of Confederate Gen. Isaac Trimble, who was injured and captured at Gettysburg, is decorated with inlaid brass.

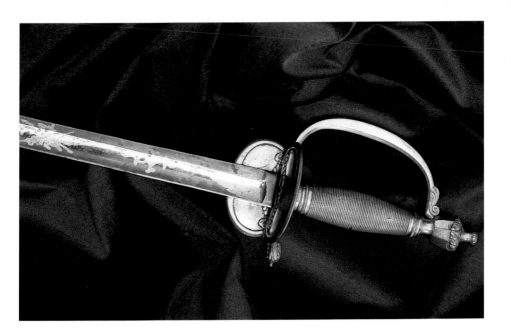

From Parties To Patient Care

The Patriot Daughters of Lancaster, a volunteer group, write of their assistance to the wounded.

"It was about ten o'clock in the morning before we entered Gettysburg, and a more distressing scene can hardly be described. Every house was a hospital, and through the open doors and windows were seen wounded men in every attitude. People were going from house to house with hasty steps and distressed countenances, as though their whole business was to care for these poor sufferers. Long trains of ambulances were conveying the less severely wounded to the depot, and those who were able, were hobbling along on their crutches as

Below: A bronze medal made from a captured Confederate cannon sold for relief efforts during the Civil War.

men were unwilling to return with their charge to the farm house from which he had been removed. To relieve their embarrassment, Father offered to care for the prisoner during the night.... The prisoner proved to be Major General Trimble, a distinguished engineer officer of Lee's army, who had lost a leg during the engagement. The men promised to return the next morning and send him on his way, but as they did not, he was taken from the parlor to a properly furnished bedroom upstairs.

The room adjoining the one in which he was placed was occupied by a young officer of our own army whose arm had been badly shattered. The poor fellow would not permit the surgeon to amputate and afterwards died from the effects of his wound.

General Trimble proved

Above: Blue bowl with U.S. Army spoon, artifacts from J. Howard Wert's childhood Gettysburg home which served as a hospital during Battle.

to be a delightful and appreciative guest. He was an elderly man, fond of children and my little sisters were frequent visitors to his room and helped to

relieve the tedium of his confinement. He was attended by his aide, a young lieutenant from Baltimore, and by his orderly named Frank. The latter proved a source of entertainment for me, for he had been a sailor, an experience that spelled romance. One day in the privacy of the stable he took off his shirt and showed me his back on which a full rigged ship was tattooed, a very unusual and thrilling exhibit.

53.

Red rebel belt with cap box, Richmond musket, soldier's photograph and cartridge wrapper from Richmond arsenal were common equipment that littered the Battlefield.

My mother ministered to both the wounded men with the best she could offer but certain citizens were displeased at the idea of a Rebel receiving such care and complained to the authorities. After a stay of two weeks their efforts to have him removed were successful, and against the repeated protests of the indignant general he was removed to the general hospital in the Theological Seminary. Some time after this exchange he sent Mother a handsome silver soup ladle, inscribed, "General Trimble to Mrs. McCurdy. The tribute of a grateful heart."

A Battered Landscape

Soon after the battle, when little had been done to change the appearance of the field, beyond the removal of the wounded and the hasty burial of the dead, I was taken *best they could. Rebel prisoners, in squads of two or three hundred, with picks and spades, were starting out, under guard, to bury their dead.*

"Into the midst of all this confusion and excitement we were ushered, not knowing whether we should find any charitable enough to give us a night's lodgings, or whether we could even find a spot on which to unload our supplies.

"Houses demolished, fences destroyed, tall forest trees mowed down like so many stalks of hemp; artillery wagons crushed, broken muskets scattered in every direction, unused cartridges in immense numbers, balls of all kinds, ramrods and bayonets, bits of clothing, belts, gloves, knapsacks, letters in great quantities, all lying promiscuously on the field; dead horses in great numbers, some torn almost asunder by cannon balls, some pierced in the side by grape shot

over parts of the Union line, to Culp's Hill, which showed evidence of terrific fighting. On the crest breastworks protected the Union soldiers, the slope was heavily wooded and many great granite boulders were scattered about. The foliage of the trees for twenty feet above the ground had been shot to pieces, showing how wild and excited the Union fire had been. On every boulder, many splotches of lead showed where a bullet had struck. I saw a long trench filled in with fresh earth, and on a blazed tree nearby, this inscription written with a pencil: "Forty Rebs buried to the right."

Near Round Top we went into a barn in which were many Confederate wounded. They lay on the threshing floor, each on a single blanket, without covering of any kind. It was too early for organized relief. They had received no [a batch of miniature iron balls shot from a cannon], and others with their legs completely shot away; some noble chargers apparently kneeling in death, their necks, crested with flowing manes, gracefully arched, as if still proud of the riders on their backs. And then many of the human dead, whose mutilated bodies, still unburied, were lying around in all positions. Some with their hands gently folded on their breasts, others reclining gracefully on their elbows, and others still leaning against trees, stumps or stones, as if wrapped in the arms of sleep, and given over to sweet dreams."

"When our patients were washed and dressed, and placed in their new beds, with a fresh pillow under their heads, and a sheet thrown over them, they looked their gratitude, which was more eloquent than words. One of us handed them each a

Equipment used in makeshift hospitals were a kit of scalpels, medicine bottles and tins from Pannier and a boxed irrigator to cleanse wounds.

handkerchief wet with cologne, and we left them to make arrangements for their supper. Already it was in progress: the tea was already made, and the buttered toast smoking on the stove, and with some nice jelly, kindly sent by those at home, the supper was complete; we took it over and gave it to each. Many, having lost their right arm, had to be fed; while some, tempting though the meal was, were too sick to partake of it; all, however, even those suffering worst, thanked us over and over again, and could scarcely be made to believe that we were to remain some weeks here, and that they were to be our special care. They all said that they had never met with such kindness, and that that meal had been the first glimpse of home life they had enjoyed since they entered the service two years ago. Thus ended our first day's experience in our new and trying vocation."

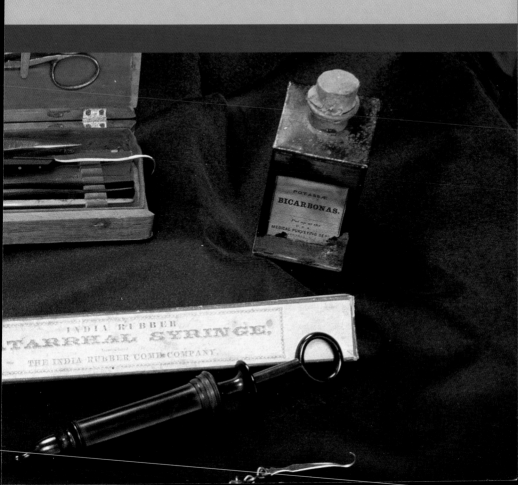

A Farm Tenant's Loss

"...those dead bodies...are still lying around my house.... I would give ten

hundred dollars if I had it if I was back on you place and fixed

as I was on the 29th of June. I had a fair prospect before me for a good

summer crop but all is gone."

"I suppose you would like to know where I am living and how I

am living. I am in Dr. Schumucker's house rent free for two or three months

and living I may almost say on nothing. We have some bread

butter and Molasse to eat .... I am at a great loss for a horse and

wagon for I can not get one wen I want one to hale rails to the

Below: These words and a flame that burns constantly mark the Eternal Light Peace Memorial.

care, and were a pitiful and dreadful sight. One of their chaplains, in uniform, was ministering to them as best he could....

Battle Relics

During the succeeding weeks I roamed over the fields with other boys looking

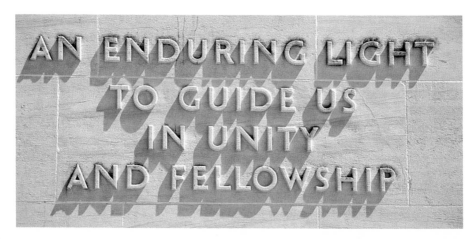

AN ENDURING LIGHT TO GUIDE US IN UNITY AND FELLOWSHIP

proper place. I hitch myself to the wheel barrow... ."

- August 10, 1863 letter of tenant John Slentz to Edward McPherson, owner of

a farm that was devastated on the first day of the battle.

bove: The base of a canister that held iron balls shot from cannons to break up enemy charges was
fired along the 11th Corps line north of Gettysburg on July 1, 1863.

for relics of various kinds, gathering a store of bullets, particularly prizing those that had been fired and had hit a boulder or a tree, giving them grotesque shapes; making collections of shells and other things dear to a boy. In our wanderings we saw many gruesome sights that cannot be described -- enough to destroy whatever glamour war may have had for us.

For inquisitive boys searching diligently in out of the way places, [there were] many dreadful evidences of the struggle. There was no lack of relics, as we called bullets and shells and grapeshot, and certain parts of the equipment of a soldier. Sword bayonets were particularly prized, for they were not in general use. We had been warned not to experiment with shells that had not exploded for they were dangerous. Two boys that I knew were killed in trying to open

Extended Courage

"I know not how men could have fought more desperately, exhibited more coolness or contested the field with more determined courage." These words of Lieutenant Colonel George F. McFarland, a principal from McAlisterville, reflect his pride in the valor of the 151st Regiment from the Keystone State on July 1. He recruited Company D, consisting largely of instructors and students from his own school, McAlisterville Academy in Juniata County. More than half of the regiment of 466 men and 21 officers fell.

Unfortunately, during one heavy volley of artillery fire, MacFarland himself was hit and his legs severely wounded. One was amputated on the field, and the other

Below: This Civil War flag's design emphasizes national unification.

mangled one pained the officer for the rest of his life. One of his friends, J. B. Bachelder, wrote a letter telling how McFarland endured prolonged suffering throughout their 28 years of friendship. "Over fifty pieces of splintered bone worked themselves out, or were extracted by the surgeon." McFarland's wife daily dressed an open sore on his leg, cheerfully attending to his needs for more than a quarter of a century. "A man of wonderful energy and willpower, [McFarland] worked to maintain his family, hobbling about..., pursuing his business affairs against all obstacles."
–from the George F. McFarland Papers.

Above: Lt. Col. George F. McFarland (1833-1892) poses prior to July 1863 when he lost the use of both legs.

them. Great stacks of muskets that had been thrown aside were piled like cordwood on the streets.

Immediately after the battle, field hospitals were erected for both the Union and the Confederate wounded. I went often to our general hospital which was a village of tents...One of Father's Baltimore friends whose sympathies were with the South, hoping to afford some solace to the forlorn wounded of the Southern Army, sent him a quantity of smoking tobacco and a number of pipes of various designs for distribution among them.

It was a busy and exciting summer that followed for thousands of visitors flocked to Gettysburg; our relics were in great demand, for everybody wanted a souvenir. But soon autumn came, and school began, and ended my adventures.

SOURCES

Alleman, Tillie Pierce, "During the Third Day of the Battle,"**What A Girl Saw and Heard of the Battle: A True Narrative.** New York: W. Lake Borland, 1889. Facsimile available at Library, Gettysburg National Military Park, Gettysburg.

Aughinbaugh, Nellie E. **Personal Experiences of a Young Girl during the Battle of Gettysburg**, inscribed by her daughter Louie Dale Leeds, published privately sometime after 1926. Used by permission.

Broadhead, Sallie Robbins, The Diary of a Lady of Gettysburg, PA from June 15 to July 15, 1863, not published, Henry E. Huntington Library & Art /Gallery, San Marino, CA. p. 17. Used by permission.

Coco, Gregory A. "The Heroism of Abner Webb," **On the Bloodstained Field.** Gettysburg: Thomas Publications, 1987, p. 27. Used by permission.

Meyer, Eugene L. "The Odyssey of Private Rosetta Wakeman, Union Army," **Smithsonian**

Magazine, Jan 1994, vol. 24, number 10, p. 100.

McCurdy, Charles M. **Gettysburg: A Memoir.**
printed for family and friends by Reed & Witting
Company, 1929. Used by permission of J.
Howard Wert Gettysburg Collection, p. 3 - 61pp.

McFarland, George F. Papers submitted by his
family to Library, Gettysburg National Military
Park. Used by permission.

Patriot Daughters of Lancaster. **Hospital Scenes
After the Battle of Gettysburg, July 1863.**
Gettysburg: G. C. Caba, reprinted 1993. Used
by permission.

Slentz, John. letter of August 10, 1863. Civilian
accounts, Adams County Historical Society.

Stumpf, Emma Yount, letter of Feb 17, 1943,
Adams County Historical Society. Used
by permission.

Wert, J. Howard **Historical Souvenir of the
Fiftieth Anniversary of the Battle of
Gettysburg July 1-4, 1913**, Harrisburg:
Harrisburg Telegraph, 1913.

The End